To _Betsy_

with love + prayers

From _Susan_

Brighter Days
Are On the Way

Illustrated by Becky Kelly

Written by Patrick Regan

Andrews McMeel Publishing

Kansas City

www.beckykelly.com

04 05 06 07 08 EPB 10 9 8 7 6 5 4 3 2 1

ISBN: 0-7407-4703-7

Illustrations by Becky Kelly
Design by Stephanie R. Farley
Edited by Polly Blair
Production by Elizabeth Nuelle

Brighter Days
Are On the Way

For you from me, with lots of TLC.

Feel better, Pate.
XXOOXX Mom

When I learned that you weren't feeling well . . .

I wanted to ride to your rescue . . .

or wave a magic wand to make you better right now!

'Cause it's just not right
that someone as good as you
should have to feel bad . . .
even for a little while.

I know I can't take away the hurt,
but there is something I can do . . .

I can remind you what a good friend
and amazing person you are,

how much you mean to so many people,

and how much we all appreciate
the light you bring to our lives.

I'm not sure if you know this or not,
but right at this moment good wishes,
positive thoughts, and healing prayers
are being sent to you from all directions.

So pull those wishes all around you like
a warm, wooly blanket.
Then, close your eyes and think about
all the wonderful things that await you . . .

long walks in the fresh air,

lively talks with close friends,

sunny spring days . . .
and night skies filled with a million stars—
each one a wish waiting to be made.

I know it's especially hard for someone like you—
someone who normally does so much—
to be held down,

but please, please try to rest and relax
and let this pass so you can be back on your feet—

and feel like your old self again.
(I'm quite fond of that old self, you know.)

Until then, keep joy in your heart . . .
and something beautiful in sight,

and treat yourself to an extra helping
of your favorite treat.
(After all, you have been very
brave and good, haven't you?)

Before you know it, you'll be ready again for fun,
laughter, and new adventures.
And when you are, I'll be ready too . . .

to help you celebrate the brighter days that lie ahead.

~ Luv U ~